Journey

Rehaan Mahmood

BookLeaf
Publishing

India | USA | UK

Presentation by *BookLeaf Publishing*

Web: www.bookleafpub.com

E-mail: info@bookleafpub.com

ISBN: 9789357444088

First edition 2022

Expression

I put pen to paper,
When I need to express,
I put pen to paper,
When I'm struggling with a test,
I put pen to paper,
When my heart bleeds,
I put pen to paper,
To plant my seeds,
I put pen to paper,
To increase my deeds,
I put pen to paper,
To spread the truth,
I put pen to paper,
Because that's what poets do,
I put pen to paper,
To cut myself loose.

Confession

I cry my tears into a pen,
To write my story,
I remorse through words,
So, we can learn,
I'm in a constant battle,
I struggle to stay firm,
Inside of me is a ball of fire,
I'm scared that I'll burn,
I just want to stop time,
Because I feel so confined,
Like my foot stuck on a mine,
My life on the verge of destruction,
My chest becomes so heavy,
The feeling of suffocation,
I just want to run away,
I'm not talking about a vacation,
I inhale memories from the past,
It's like mental intoxication,
Remembrance in Allah,
Is my only medication,
I bleed out these words on paper,
Call it my confession,
But I don't call my trails a burden,
By my Lord I have learnt my lesson.

Lost

When you look at me,
I look well put together,
But internally,
I'm lost and confused,
like the British weather,
When I look in the mirror,
I don't like what I see,
I see a foolish man,
Who accepted defeat,
Now I'm crawling around,
Trying to get back up on my feet,
Sometimes I just enter my mind,
Then take a seat,
Watch all of my agony and mistakes,
On repeat,
The only escape is to just sleep,
Yeah, I always sleep to escape the pain,
Then I wake in silence,
Whilst living in a world of voices,
So many whispers,
There're no such thing as easy choices,
Movement is too fast,
I just want to slow it down,
Can't get peace and quiet,
But there's no one around,

Can't escape my imaginary shackles,
The key is yet to be found,
I want to just fly away,
But I'm tied to the ground,
I tell myself to stand up and fight,
Anxiousness covers me,
Like gloomy clouds in the daylight,
Feel so much emptiness,
Like no stars at night,
I just pray,
I pray that the Almighty,
Gives me might.

Painful Hope

This pain that has been hidden,
Hidden by dark shadows and gloomy nights,
Always finds it's way to my path,
In order to take away my sight,
I try so hard to turn on my torch,
But every time it consumes the light,
In joyful times it tries it's best to blur out
delight,
It's a constant battle,
Like I'm a full-time knight,
No shining armour,
Just a tiresome fight,
It's like a glass ceiling,
Ready to stop me from reaching any height,
I'm pushing,
And I will keep pushing,
I just don't know how long I can keep this
might,
But I'm no runaway,
I will hold on,
With hardship will come ease,
So, my Lord is the one I call upon,
Changing my life around before my soul is gone.

Wounds

These wounds that have healed,
begin to bleed again,
But remember we are not supposed to,
Live in harmony until the end,
Hidden in every trial,
There's a blessing that He sends,
With every person that is absent,
He places one that will attend,
No matter how distant you have been,
He will remind you again and again,
every time you turn your back on him,
He will always forgive,
All He asks from us in return,
Is by his name we live.

Why?

Why do I feel so lost?
Whilst I hold a map of directions,
I continue to walk,
whilst I know the route for correction,
I make too many mistakes,
I have an everlasting collection,
My heart is torn apart,
But I don't give it the right affection,
I've started to build steel walls,
My defence is under construction,
I try to rebuild from the aftermath,
But it seems I struggle to do the maths,
Even if I do find X I'm always stuck on why,
Cut off my wings when I tried to fly,
Left me to drown knowing I can't swim,
But with struggle,
You can reach a deeper connection within,
Knowing He will never leave,
So, you call upon Him,
Why?
Because I lost connection,
With the embodiment of perfection.

Growth

With every trial I have grown,
I've broke through so many thorns,
That's why,
I always get back up on my own,
I fall so much,
But that's not what I've shown,
I'm wearing a mask,
That's made out of stone,
That's why no matter the numbers,
I'll always feel alone,
I know so many care for me
And if I ever needed them,
They'd always be there, undoubtedly,
So, I ask you to please forgive me,
I never let you in,
Even though you ask consistently,
But when everything looks so dark,
I can't see clearly,
I wanted to call out,
But I rejected myself subconsciously,
Sometimes you just have to break down,
And ask for Gods help sincerely,
Only then,
You may feel a high level of serenity,
So, this was all God's plan,

A means of guidance,
To becoming a better man.

3am Thoughts

Left alone just my pen and my paper,
Mindful thoughts, be it minor or major,
The devils' whispers getting stronger,
I try my best to avoid my demons,
But they're taking over my mind like an invader,
My chest becomes tight,
I struggle to breathe,
Internal screams,
I just want the devil to leave,
But my mind keeps racing,
Like why did I wear my heart on my sleeve,
Easy access, they ripped it off,
Left it to bleed,
Anxiety triggered, I didn't know what I need,
So, I picked up my lord's book,
"With hardship will come ease"
So, I continued to read,
"With hardship will come ease"
So, I tell myself,
The sun will rise after the night dies,
When the sun falls,
Upon my lord I will call,
A conversation with Him is all I need,
I know they'll still be scars,
But at least now they won't bleed.

Internal War

Broken does not even define how I feel,
On my mind and heart, I have a seal,
It's like words can't explain this torment,
A shattered heart and an enslaved mind,
Its like any good I do is undermined,
Because the wrong I do will always outshine,
I may as well be in a casket,
Because I am dead inside,
I'm alone even though I have many by my side,
I tell myself it's just in my mind,
You don't know how many times I've tried,
I don't know if I can handle another tide,
Will I ever see another sunrise?
I've had enough of these sleepless nights,
I've had enough of these internal wars,
I can no longer fight,
My heart no longer has the might,
My eyes can no longer see the light,
My mind sometimes scares me,
It's like I'm my own enemy,
My thoughts are so destructive,
It leaves my body captive,
The devil always making this world attractive,
I always end up losing myself,

No matter how much I try to practice,
Slowly I'm breaking,
My world is shaking,
My purpose is disappearing,
My smile I'm always faking,
But nothing can ever change my belief,
That my wings will also grow,
That the light will show,
Just like the night snow,
My world will have colour,
Like a beautiful rainbow,
Also, it's alright to feel low,
But always rise after every blow,
No matter what happens,
Know that the blessings will arrive,
Just how everyday ends with the sunset,
How every night end with a sunrise,
After the rain the puddles will dry,
Blessings will come, no need to cry,
But if you really need to heal,
Let your tears reveal the pain,
Because sometimes you need to cry,
So, your thoughts don't drive you insane,
If your journey begins to lose direction,
Make sure you catch the next train,
Get back up and fight, again and again,
So, I believe, no, I know,
Whatever happens is what God decrees,
Whatever God decrees is good for me.

So, for every blessing I will be thankful,
For every hardship I will be grateful,
For He is teaching me a lesson,
For God is the most insightful,
Never be afraid to turn back to Him,
The most merciful.

Blade

I hold this blade to my skin,
Because I want to release the pain from within,
I want to engrave my mistakes,
so, I don't commit them again,
Me and my blade, we know each other,
Were good friends,
Every time I'm upset, he embraces my skin,
So, I can bleed out the pain,
But he always throws it in my face,
Because these scars will remain,
Like every bad situation is framed,
On the wall for everyone to see,
But this friend cut me too deep,
That it haunts me in my own sleep,
So, I drop the blade,
And I let this friendship fade,
Because there's nothing worse than a toxic
friend,
He will never help you mend,
Turn to God for His hands will always extend.

Routes

They say you haven't walked a mile in my
shoes,
But everyone walks a different route,
I'm just saying,
God gives different trials to me and you,
He doesn't Burden a soul,
More than what he can bear,
The strength you have,
You are not even aware,
Injustice is not in God's nature,
Known as the most just and fair,
The way He plans,
We cannot understand,
But maybe that trial,
Has given you the strength to withstand,
After a hard fall the will to stand,
Just keep pushing and remember,
Your fate is within God's hand.

Hidden Blessings

I remember my mind was clustered.
My trials leaving me flustered,
Couldn't see no day light just rain,
Dark clouds covering the joy, like pain,
There were no stars in the sky,
No stargazing even if I tried,
But it was my own distress,
That left me so blind,
The day was just waiting for me,
To rise like the sun,
I couldn't change the past,
What's done has been done,
Just repent to God and move on,
You will see the stars,
Just open your eyes,
Look past the mist of lies,
That the devil made you see,
So you would compromise,
Don't let the trials be the reason,
For you to complain,
Just take God's name,
And look for the blessings they contain.

Imperfection

I'm not perfect I have many imperfections,
So many mistakes,
but from them I've learnt lessons,
I use my scars as my motivation,
I mean there's good in every bad situation,
People around me changed,
So, it became a form of inspiration,
Trying everyday to make the right decisions,
Allah sent down His guidance,
So, now I bow down in submission,
Live to only please my lord,
Is my number one mission,
And its okay if you focus starts to drift,
As even the light isn't clear in the mist,
This deen is hard to hold in your fists,
Like that of hot coal,
But its worth more than gold,
Have big dreams,
that's what we're told,
So, aim for heaven, now that's goals,
have patience in every hardship,
and your blessings will unfold,
don't run after the dunya,
like your soul has been sold,
be true to yourself,

remain beautiful and bold,
I know this life is like a rollercoaster,
And you can't always take control,
But remembrance in God,
Should be your protocol,
Like when in distress,
Who is better to call,
Then the one who hears all,
And sometimes when you fall,
It's hard to even crawl,
Having Allah by your side,
Is all you need to stand tall,
It's crazy, your head to the ground,
Is where your light can be found,
In the lowest position,
When no one is even around,
But your inner self is sound,
And remembrance in God is our strength,
Trust in Him can get you to any length,
Anyone can be taken by darkness,
This world can make us anxious,
Forgetting our morals,
Like we got no conscious,
But we are not hopeless,
Remember God is with us,
He can show us the light,
That would leave our eyes wide open,
He can keep us calm,
Like the sounds of the ocean,

All he asks for us,
Is to live with devotion,
Our Rab will always have the solution.

Conflicted

I feel like a cloud follows me everywhere I go,
The light is hard to see,
The darkness is bound to follow,
I really want to do good,
But my heart is just hollow,
Emptiness can make you drown,
Even if the water is shallow,
Always seeing black and white,
Whist the photo is in colour,
Not recognising pain,
Like he's disguised as another,
Because every time he knocks on the door,
I put my weakness on show,
Like I'm in a battlefield with no cover,
Or in a war with no armour,
So, I got pierced by the blade that I mentally
made,
I feel like I'm beginning to fade,
Metaphorically maybe even mentally,
I feel like I'm about to lose myself,
Maybe being nice isn't good for your health,
Maybe I just can't change,
Or priorities need to be rearranged,
Maybe this is all wisdom with its teaching,
Full of lessons and my soul is feeding,

All I can do is trust in the process,
Just worry about my progress,
Keep my Lord's words in my heart,
And firm that this dunya,
Won't tear me apart.

Puppet

Life is so mad,
No one is ever real,
It's like the mask has to be pealed,
In order for their true faces to be revealed,
How can you be so fake?
How many people did you break?
You can't stand there and call this a mistake,
For God's sake just end the explanation,
Because there's no reason for your heartless
actions,
Do you even recognise your own reflection?
Your not what you say not even a fraction,
Then you lie and deceive for your own
satisfaction,
There're too many cold people,
They'll hurt you then come back for a sequel,
You never knew because you thought their love
was equal,
It'll hit you so deep that you want to believe it's
a lie,
So, you begin to make excuses in your mind,
But this mirage doesn't last, for every night you
cry,
For every morning you wake with tears in your
eyes,

Like who knew the thing that kept me going,
Would become the pain that keeps me grieving,
All the happy thoughts in my mind,
I now know they were deceiving,
It seems to me that my motivation is leaving,
I feel so much right now that I just pray to stop
feeling,
The veil Infront of your lies is disappearing,
So, your true self is revealing,
You had me on strings, well played,
Now I'm struggling to let these feeling fade,
My colourful future has now become greyed,
Who knew that you had the power to cut deeper
than a blade,
So, I'm just in this heartbreak haze,
This broken faze, this lonely craze,
From these memories I cannot erase,
Our future that won't take place,
Because of your hidden face,
So, He removed you without a trace,
To God, I send all praise.

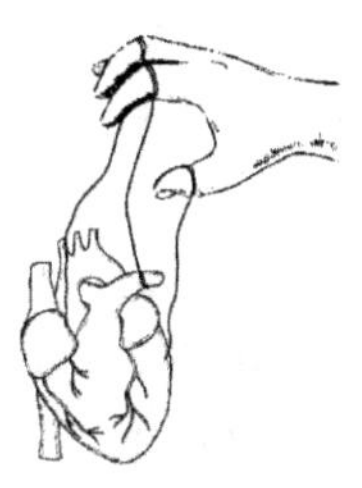

Snakes

Life is trying its best to make me fall apart,
My heart been broken so many times,
I'm struggling to find the parts,
A big piece of me is lost,
Slowly my heart is turning into frost,
Grey clouds covering me in vain,
Every single rain drop resembles my pain,
My eyes full of weakness and tearful stains,
An anger so deep it keeps my mind stained,
My eyes filled with a fiery rage,
Secluding myself from the world,
For it is not time to engage,
People always judging the whole book,
Whilst only reading a page,
These snakes were hiding in the crowd,
people threw the bait,
Now they are hissing out loud,
Whist I look from my bird's eye view,
Knowing from these trials I can pull through,
Because when I have my Lord by my side,
There's no harm you can do,
After I release my tears in prayer to him,
I leave my supplication with a wide grin,
Because when I confide in my Rab,
My soul is cleansed from within.

Snatched

All my dreams were within reach,
But dreams weren't meant for me,
I don't even want to hear anyone preach,
I really just want to sleep,
Because there's no point in dreaming,
When it always leaves me empty,
I remember it like it was yesterday,
Was holding you in my palms,
Tears in my eyes, my world was in my arms,
I could finally rest and feel calm,
Because you were my ray of light,
Be it day or be it night,
You were my rainbow after the storm,
Whilst the world kept me cold,
Your presence made me warm,
When you used to sleep on my chest,
I finally felt like I was at peace
For having you in my life I was blessed,
You were the answer to all my prayers,
Until one day I woke,
It was like constant nightmares,
I was stuck on a road with no streetlight,
I lost all my hope I was struggling to fight,
You were snatched from me that night,
Its like my heart was ripped from my chest,

I was broken, didn't know how to deal with this
test,
The world was weighing down on me,
The storm returned slowly,
The rainbow also left me,
I wanted to give you what I never had,
I just wanted to make you happy whenever
you're sad,
I just wanted you to confide in your dad,
I wanted to be the father I never had,
But I will never let this stop me,
I will always fight to be in the presence of your
light,
To be with you I will drop everything,
I will always look forward to pushing you on the
swing,
I will always be here to watch you grow,
Can't wait for the first time we play in the snow,
When life gets hard and you don't know where
to go,
I'll always lend you a helping hand,
Whenever you fall, I will always help you to
stand,
Daddy will always love you,
I hope one day you will understand.

09.19

This numbness running through my veins,
The demon I locked away,
Has broken his chains,
I'm sitting in silence,
Trying not to complain,
Feeling suffocated,
Trying to hide this pain,
With every single breath,
My heart feels compressed,
A day without you,
Is like an arrow through my chest,
You are my reason why,
You will grow to be my ride or die,
I dream of being reunited with you,
I talk about you to the most high,
Every minute of the day,
Every single night,
Saying your name giving gives me a reason to
fight,
You are my world,
And I love you,
My baby girl.

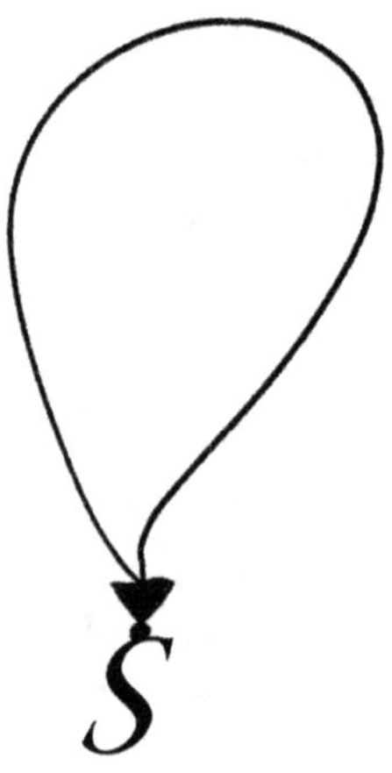

Guidance

I remember what I used to be,
A lost soul that couldn't see,
Depression left me hazy,
No self-love,
I didn't want to be me,
Couldn't fit in,
I just wanted to be happy,
So, I lost myself,
which affected me deeply,
character changed completely,
mind so clustered,
that I couldn't think clearly,
ran away,
from any problem that came before me,
was never alone,
but I felt lonely,
I was distant moving away slowly,
But when I was blessed with deen,
It changed my life drastically,
Head down five times daily,
Never felt this level of serenity,
I swear this guidance is heavenly,
Still slip up,
But relying on His mercy,
Changed mindset,

Full of positivity,
Blessed with a few brothers,
Who are like my family,
Blood always supporting me,
Thank Allah for all that He blessed me,
For fixing the pieces,
Whilst the dunya gone and broke me,
So, my younger self,
I'm sorry for not seeing with clarity,
But I wouldn't take it back,
For that is what made me.

Freedom

Move like the wind,
Free and powerful, with an aura calmness,
Dancing with the rain like a symphony,
Droplets of tears,
Planting seeds of hope inside of me,
From the pain of my own actions,
To calling out for my Lord's mercy,
Having trust in Him,
Like the leaves,
That sway with the cool breeze.